RABBITS!

A MY INCREDIBLE WORLD PICTURE BOOK

MY INCREDIBLE WORLD

Copyright © 2018, My Incredible World

All rights reserved. This book or any portion thereof may not be reproduced or used in any manner whatsoever without the express written permission of the copyright holder.

www.myincredibleworld.com

Photos Credits
Page 1. By Peter Lloyd, available at https://unsplash.com/photos/tT1ZifjJ9fs
Page 2. By Andrea Reiman, available at https://unsplash.com/photos/OmIAWzvvViU
Page 3. By Shirui Cheng, available at https://unsplash.com/photos/VvfXgiuz4v4
Page 4. By Davies Designs, available at https://unsplash.com/photos/rdoqU8NTaM4
Page 5. By Chan Swan, available at https://unsplash.com/photos/y0U6hWulUi0
Page 6. By Matthew Kosloski, available at https://unsplash.com/photos/mKfgOMYTttU
Page 7. By Steve Harvey, available at https://unsplash.com/photos/HCRHHnmUxl0
Page 8. By Ray Hennessy, available at https://unsplash.com/photos/Mw46Q41UfZ8
Page 9. By Nathan Anderson, available at https://unsplash.com/photos/qZJajnlnPSw
Page 10. By Vincent van Zalinge, available at https://unsplash.com/photos/nq5bgxSg8gE
Page 11. By Caleb Woods, available at https://unsplash.com/photos/im7bmQ_nWd0
Page 12. By David Solce, available at https://unsplash.com/photos/PhOAIvz3fBA
Page 13. By Chan Swan, available at https://unsplash.com/photos/iVm9hTDx2ww
Page 14. By Leximphoto, available at https://unsplash.com/photos/UqM8A0sgVZk
Page 15. By Eric Ward, available at https://unsplash.com/photos/euPteOH9KFU
Page 16. By Gustavo Zambelli, available at https://unsplash.com/photos/Ep_IYAGK51w
Page 17. By Maxi, available at https://unsplash.com/photos/Rp9GS9PLFr4
Page 18. By Jennifer Chen, available at https://unsplash.com/photos/h0GbJwpMNiM
Page 19. By Michael Roubos, available at https://unsplash.com/photos/jB47hKBU4KE
Page 20. By Gavin Allanwood, available at https://unsplash.com/photos/hcxqLJjI99E
Page 21. By Maxi, available at https://unsplash.com/photos/fipJx4M8TsE
Page 22. By Waranya Mooldee, available at https://unsplash.com/photos/Efj0HGPdPKs

There are about 14 million pet rabbits in the world and even more in the wild!

There are over 300 breeds of pet rabbits throughout 70 countries!

More than half of the world's rabbits live in North America!

Rabbits are the 3rd most popular pet in the U.S. after cats and dogs.

Rabbits are very intelligent, social, and clean animals!

Wild rabbits live underground with up to 30 others in burrows called **warrens**.

Rabbits have long ears that can pick up sounds from up to 2 miles away!

Rabbits are usually farsighted, but they can see almost 360 degrees!

Rabbits are **herbivores**, meaning they eat only grasses and other plants.

Rabbits can run between 25 and 45 miles per hour!

Rabbits can weigh between 2.5 and 20 pounds, depending on the breed!

A baby rabbit is called a **kit**, a female is called a **doe**, and a male is a **buck**.

Some rabbits have short hair and some have long hair!

Rabbits' whiskers are as long as their bodies are wide, just like cats!

Wild rabbits usually live up to 2 years, but pet rabbits can live up to 10!

Rabbits have an excellent sense of smell!

Rabbits have 28 teeth that never stop growing!

Rabbits chew about 120 times per minute, which keeps their teeth short.

Mother rabbits usually have litters of 4 to 12 kits.

Rabbits can have hundreds of children and grandchildren in their lifetime!

A group of rabbits is callled a **herd**.

Rabbits are incredible!

Made in United States
North Haven, CT
21 March 2023